Sew Simple Lo

Karin Hellaby

Quilters Haven

Publications

About the author

Karin Hellaby is the owner of a quilt shop, Quilters Haven, in Suffolk UK. She is a graduate Textiles teacher who enjoys travelling and teaching all over the world.

As well as writing books, Karin has contributed articles to all the UK quilting magazines.

Karin is an adviser for Arena Travel (www.arenatravel.com), a specialist holiday company who have arranged holidays for quilters in Europe, America and New Zealand.

In 1998 Karin was the winner of the Michael Kile Scholarship and International Retailer of the Year.

Acknowledgements

My thanks to Pam, Debs, Teresa, Heather, Annie, Helen, Nicola, Pippa, Allan and Rosemary.

This book is dedicated to my eldest son Ross – whether he likes it or not!

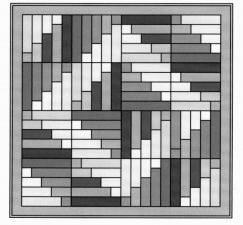

8 blocks

8 blocks

Quilt plan for Blue Heaven *(see previous page). You will find plans for most of the quilts in this book on pages 11–14.*

First published by
Quilters Haven Publications in 2008

Copyright © Karin Hellaby 2008

Graphics by Rosemary Muntus
Layout by Allan Scott

Photography by Colin Shaw Photography
Tel: +44(0)1394 387328

Printed by Borcombe SP
Premier Way, Abbey Park Industrial Estate, Romsey
Hampshire SO51 9AQ

ISBN 978-0-9540928-4-9 UPC 7-44674-44097-6
Quilters Haven Publications
68 High Street, Wickham Market
Suffolk IP13 0QU, UK

Tel: +44 (0)1728 746275
Fax: +44 (0)1728 746314

www.quilters-haven.co.uk

Introduction

This pattern booklet is designed to show you how to make log cabin-style quilts in an easy format. Using this technique there is less sewing to do – so the quilt making is much quicker – but the finished result is stunning. This simple patchwork block can be twisted, turned and multiplied to make many quilt variations. The finished patchwork block is a 10" square. The mini quilt variation uses a 5" block.

You can use a palette of two fabrics, nine fabrics or up to 18 fabrics for a 24-block quilt. And you can use 36 fabrics or even more for a 64-block quilt!

Lotus Cranes 1 (54" square) by Debs Gardner, fabric from Timeless Treasures.

Choosing fabrics

1 Each log is a narrow strip, maximum 2" finished width and 10" finished length, small-print fabrics work well.

2 For best results use 100% cotton, the sort you find in good-quality patchwork and quilting shops. The yardage is based on 42" wide fabrics.

3 Directional prints can be fun but you may find they end up flowing in every direction once you have twisted and turned those blocks!

4 Large prints work well as interesting borders.

QH tips

Fabric strips are cut straight across the bolt from selvedge to selvedge.

Stitch with a ¼" seam. Most machines have a patchwork foot which will give you the seam guide.

Pure (100%) cotton thread should be used with 100% cotton fabric.

A **strip set** is two or more strips sewn, right sides together, and pressed with the seam towards the darker fabric.

Fit a new machine needle every 6–8 hours of sewing.

Use a slightly smaller than medium length machine stitch. The stitching should be small enough not to come undone, but large enough to 'unpick' if you go wrong.

Pin at right angles to the seams; that way the fabrics won't move and it's easy to slip the pins out as you stitch towards them. I like to use fine flower pins.

Sew Simple Logs – 9 fabrics

Fabric requirements

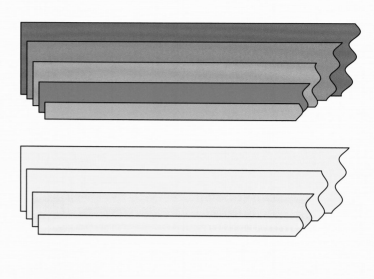

Choose nine fabrics – five darks and four lights. Cut *two* strips from each fabric to make a 40" x 60" quilt:

Dark #1	¾ yard	2 x 10½"
Dark #2	½ yard	2 x 8½"
Dark #3	½ yard	2 x 6½"
Dark #4	min. ¼ yard	2 x 4½"
Dark #5	¼ yard	2 x 2½"
Light #1	½ yard	2 x 8½"
Light #2	½ yard	2 x 6½"
Light #3	min. ¼ yard	2 x 4½"
Light #4	¼ yard	2 x 2½"

This is the easiest quilt to get started with, yet it still gives you a multi fabric effect. The 24 patchwork blocks are arranged into a traditional design known as 'barn raising'. Choose five dark fabrics and decide in which order you wish to use them. The first dark will be 'seen' most, descending to the fifth dark, which appears as a square.

You may wish to have your favourite fabric as the first dark or you may wish to have the fabrics arranged from dark to light or light to dark within the darks.

Then look at your four light fabrics and arrange them in a similar way.

1 Stitch the following strip sets using a ¼" seam. Stitch the two strips together along the long sides. Each time you will sew two identical strip sets.

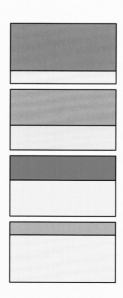

8½" dark stitched to a 2½" light

6½" dark stitched to a 4½" light

4½" dark stitched to a 6½" light

2½" dark stitched to a 8½" light

The fifth strip is the cut 10½" strip in a dark fabric.

2 Press each strip set seam towards the dark fabric. I like to use the side of the iron, pressing gently on the wrong side before the final press on the right side when I check that the seam is 'open'.

Each strip set should be 10½" wide and approximately 42" long.

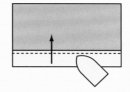

3 Straighten one end of the solid strip, before cutting the logs.

QH tip

Speed cutting will save you time at this stage. I fold the strip set in half, straighten the ends together and then cut two logs with each cut.

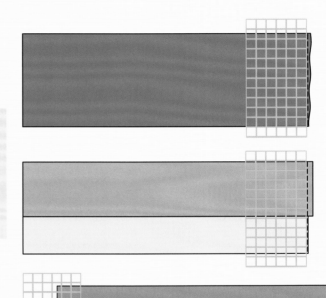

4 From *each strip set* cut twelve 2½" wide logs. From the two 10½" wide dark strips cut 24 2½" wide logs. You should have five different groups each with 24 logs.

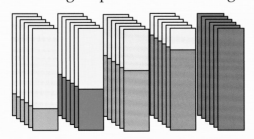

5 At this stage it is helpful to lay out five logs together to view one block. Choose one log from each of the five different groups and *place as shown here.* Eventually you will be making 24 identical blocks.

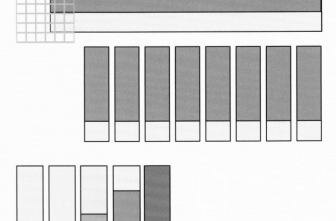

6 Pin the first two logs together, matching corners before stitching along the length. Stitch from the light end towards the dark end.

Make sure you stitch the log pairs along the same side, with the longer dark on top and towards the bottom of the log. This avoids you piecing any mirror image blocks.

7 Then stitch third and fourth logs together. Stitch log pairs together and finally add the solid log.

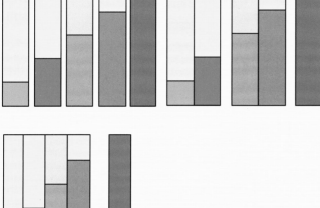
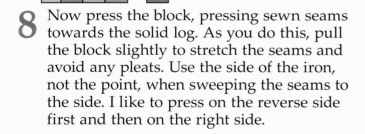

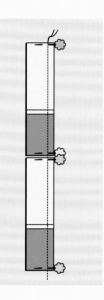
8 Now press the block, pressing sewn seams towards the solid log. As you do this, pull the block slightly to stretch the seams and avoid any pleats. Use the side of the iron, not the point, when sweeping the seams to the side. I like to press on the reverse side first and then on the right side.

9 Stitch another 23 blocks. Arrange blocks into the quilt design.

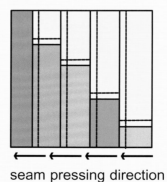

seam pressing direction

Stitch blocks together into pairs.

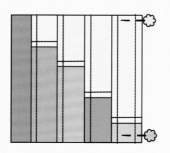

6

Then stitch the pairs into a horizontal row. Stitch all six horizontal rows.

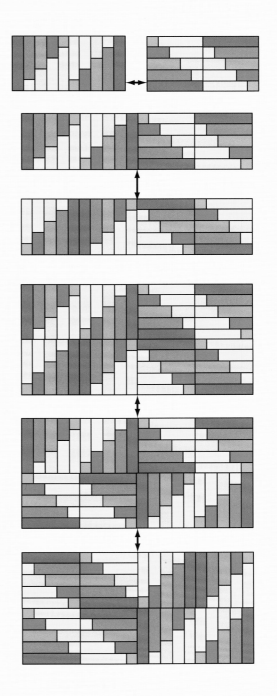

Press the new seams in one direction, alternating the direction on alternate rows. This will help the seams to nestle together when you're stitching the rows together.

Stitch horizontal quilt rows together in pairs.

Then stitch the paired rows together into the quilt top. Is the quilt top ready to be finished? Or does it need a border?

What If?

Y ou laid the quilt blocks in a different design?

Y ou looked at the many ideas in this book – and then came up with your own?

Y ou mirrored the blocks so the dark solid log is on the left-hand side?

4 blocks

8 blocks

Moon over Empress Garden by Teresa Wardlaw (43" x 54"). Uses nine fabrics chosen from the Andover Fabrics range.

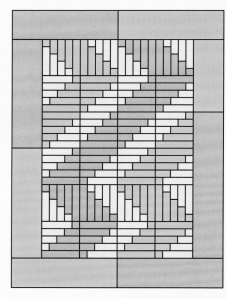

12 blocks

12 blocks

Zig Zag (27" x 37") uses hand dyed fabric by Teresa Wardlaw. Mini logs are used in this exciting three-colour design. The borders make best use of the fabric that was left over!

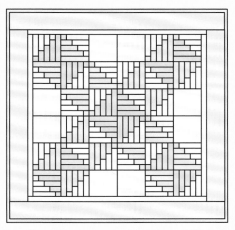

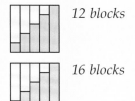
12 blocks

16 blocks

8 blocks

Love and Kisses *by Teresa Wardlaw (38" square), a mini log quilt using three fabrics and four plain fabric background squares.*

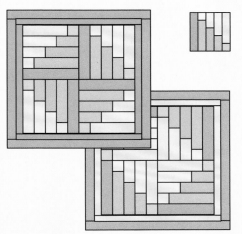

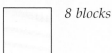
4 blocks each

Two mini log hangings by Helen Hazon (12" square) using Heming House fabrics from Moda.

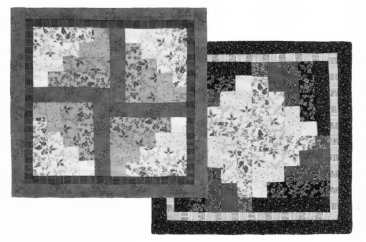

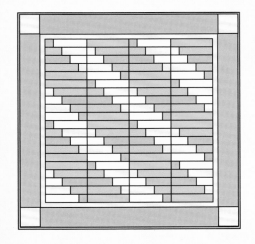

16 blocks

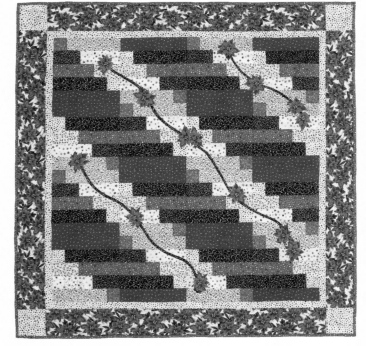

Christmas Logs and Flowers *by Annie Whatling (49" square). Made from the Christmas Wishes fabric range by Makower. Fussy cut poinsettia and vines have been appliquéd to the light log background. Uses nine fabrics.*

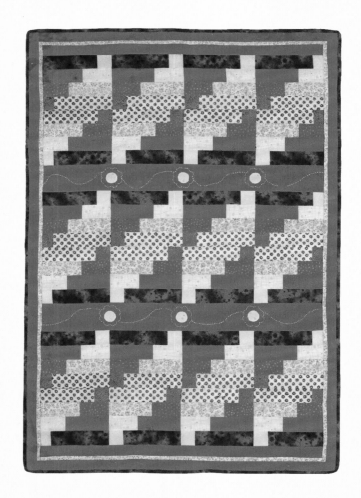

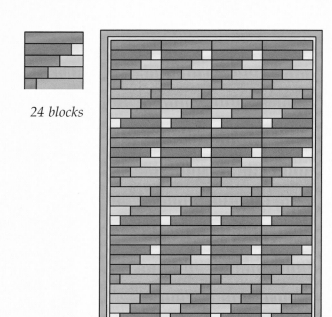

24 blocks

Electric Storm at Sunset *by Heather Babb (42" x 62").*
Incorporates appliquéd circles and sashiko quilting. Uses
nine fabrics.

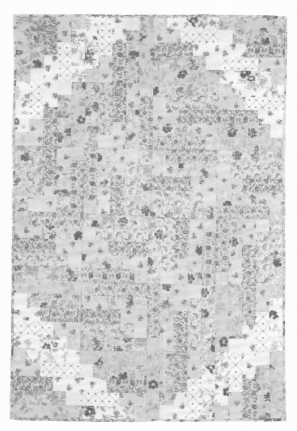

12 blocks

12 blocks

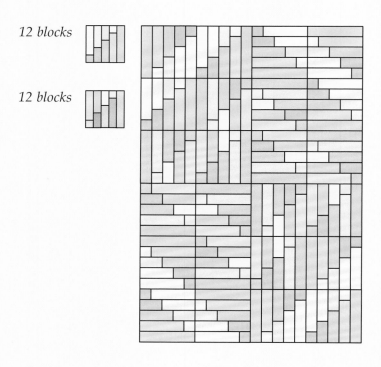

Summer Medley *by Nicola Foreman (41" x 61"), a*
barn-raising design, uses the Simplicity fabric range from
Moda. Made with 18 fabrics.

24 blocks

Lotus Circles
(53″ x 72″) by
Debs Gardner;
logs set in a
diamond design.
Uses nine
fabrics.

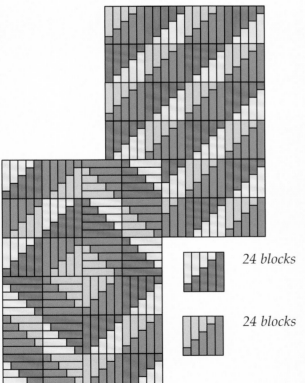

24 blocks

24 blocks

Heming House *by Helen Hazon (49″ x 80″) uses 18
fabrics from a range by Moda. The reverse of the quilt
(far right) has a diagonal stripe setting.*

11

Sew Simple Logs - 18 fabrics

Fabric requirements

This quilt has a wonderful multi-fabric effect! This time each strip set will have different fabrics. Cut one strip from each fabric to make a 40" x 60" quilt.

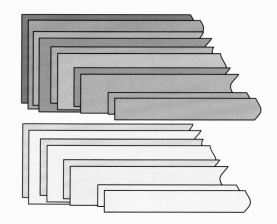

Dark #1	2 x ½ yard	10½" from each
Dark #2	2 x ¼ yard	8½" from each
Dark #3	2 x ¼ yard	6½" from each
Dark #4	2 x ¼ yard	4½" from each
Dark #5	2 x ¼ yard	2½" from each
Light #1	2 x ¼ yard	8½" from each
Light #2	2 x ¼ yard	6½" from each
Light #3	2 x ¼ yard	4½" from each
Light #4	2 x ¼ yard	2½" from each

1 Stitch the following strip sets using a ¼" seam. Stitch the two strips together along the long sides. You will have two of each sized strip set, to make in total eight strip sets.

8½" dark stitched to a 2½" light

6½" dark stitched to a 4½" light

4½" dark stitched to a 6½" light

2½" dark stitched to a 8½" light

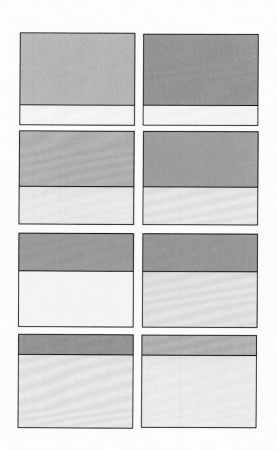

2 Press each strip set towards the dark fabric. Each one should be 10½" wide.

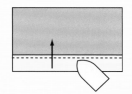

3 Straighten one end of each strip set. From each strip set cut 12 2½" pieces. From the two 10½" dark strips cut 12 2½" pieces from each.

You should have ten different groups each with 12 logs.

4 Proceed as in Sew Simple Logs from point 5 on page 6.

Make each of the 24 blocks look different from each other by randomly placing logs from each group but keeping to the light/dark colour placement.

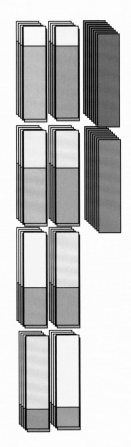

12 blocks

12 blocks

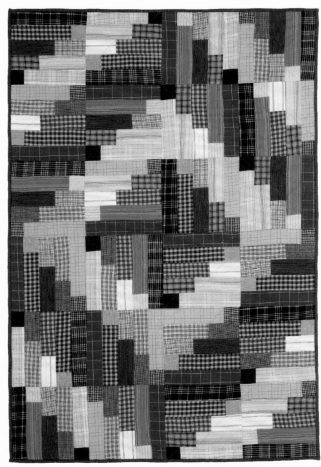

Homespun by Karin Hellaby (41" x 61") uses 18 fabrics: log squares are set in a 'barn raising' design. Note the position of the solid log in the block.

Mini Logs

Fabric requirements

The 20" x 30" mini quilt is finished with 5" blocks and logs that are only 1" wide. Only two fabrics have been used in this quilt.

Dark	½ yard	Cut five strips 5½", 4½", 3½", 2½", and 1½" wide.
Light	½ yard	Cut four strips 4½", 3½", 2½", and 1½" wide.

1 Stitch the following strip sets using a ¼" seam. Stitch the two strips together along the long sides.

4½" dark stitched to a 1½" light

3½" dark stitched to a 2½" light

2½" dark stitched to a 3½" light

1½" dark stitched to a 4½" light

The fifth strip is the cut 5½" strip in a dark fabric.

2 Press each strip set seam towards the dark fabric.

Each strip set should be 5½" wide and approximately 42" long.

3 Continue from point 3 of *Sew Simple Logs* on page 5, cutting 24 1½" logs from each strip set.

Continue from point 3 of *Sew Simple Logs* on page 5

What If?

You used four fat quarters of fabric? Use two dark and two light fabrics. Think of this as making two different blocks, twelve in each colourway.

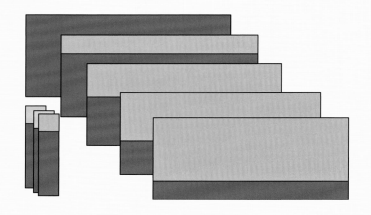

Finishing

Layering the quilt

The fabric should be 3" larger all round than your quilt top. Choose a wadding (batting) just a little smaller than your backing.

Pin out the backing wrong side up. Lay the wadding on top and finally your quilt top right side up. Keep the layers together with safety pins or a basting spray. Then quilt. The quilts in this book were all machine-quilted.

Once quilting is complete, trim the excess wadding and backing even with the quilt top. Baste the outer edge of the quilt ⅛" inside the quilt edge, to keep the edges together.

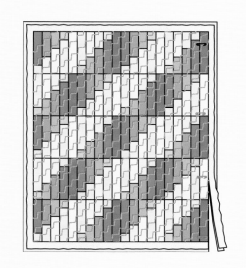

Binding

Cut enough 2½" wide strips to go all the way around the quilt with an excess of 18". Join the binding strips together with a 45-degree angle seam. Press seams open.

Fold binding in half wrong sides together and press. Cut the beginning of the binding at a 45-degree angle and turn in the edge ¼". Press.

Use a ⅜" seam allowance and a walking foot when stitching the binding to the front of the quilt. Start at the bottom edge a third of the way in from the corner, leaving a tail of 3".

Stop sewing ⅜" from the next corner and backstitch to secure the threads. Remove the quilt from the machine and cut the threads.

Fold the binding up and then down so that the fold is even with the quilt edge. Pin.

Sew down the side to the next corner. Repeat for all four corners.

As you near the start point, cut the binding strip and tuck the end into the folded beginning strip. Finish the sewing and backstitch. Blind-stitch the folded edge to the tucked strip.

Turn the binding to the back of the quilt and blind-stitch to the backing.

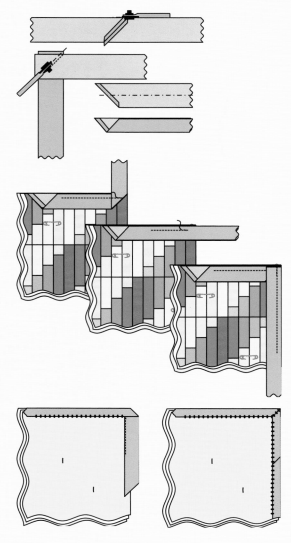

And a few ideas...

There is no limit to the ways in which this sew simple log technique can be used. You can make the log colours very similar or very different. You can use traditional log-cabin sets or make up your own. You can create all-over log designs or intersperse log-blocks with plain ones. This is such a delicious technique!

So choose your favourite fabrics right now – and let your imagination run riot!

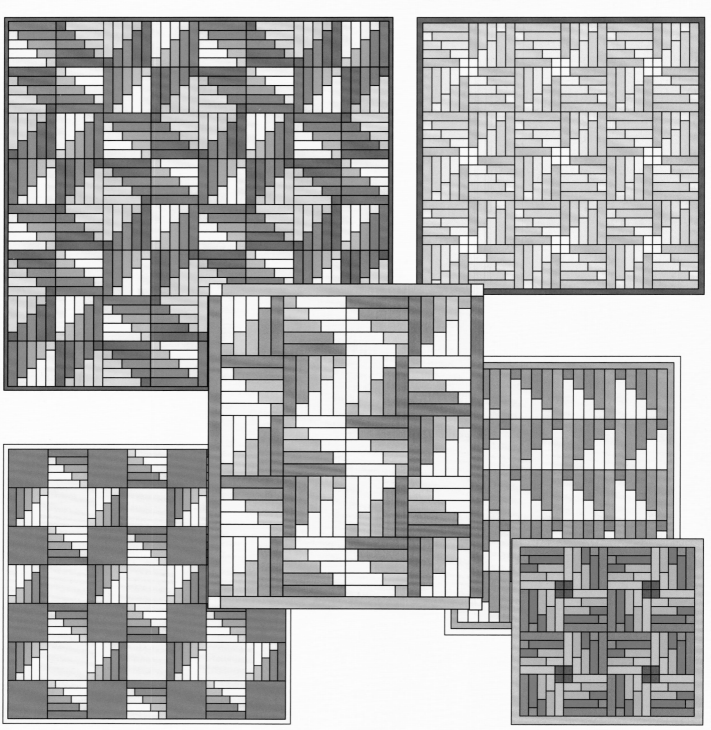